FULL THROTTLE

MONSTER TRUCKS

BY THOMAS K. ADAMSON

EPIC

BELLWETHER MEDIA • MINNEAPOLIS, MN

EPIC BOOKS are no ordinary books. They burst with intense action, high-speed heroics, and shadows of the unknown. Are you ready for an Epic adventure?

This edition first published in 2019 by Bellwether Media, Inc.

No part of this publication may be reproduced in whole or in part without written permission of the publisher. For information regarding permission, write to Bellwether Media, Inc., Attention: Permissions Department, 6012 Blue Circle Drive, Minnetonka, MN 55343.

Library of Congress Cataloging-in-Publication Data

Names: Adamson, Thomas K., 1970- author.
Title: Monster Trucks / by Thomas K. Adamson.
Description: Minneapolis, MN : Bellwether Media, Inc., 2019. | Series: Epic.
    Full Throttle | Includes bibliographical references and index. | Audience:
    Ages 7-12. | Audience: Grades 2 to 7.
Identifiers: LCCN 2018002177 (print) | LCCN 2018008128 (ebook) | ISBN
    9781626178748 (hardcover : alk. paper)| ISBN 9781681036212 (ebook)
Subjects: LCSH: Monster trucks–Juvenile literature.
Classification: LCC TL230.5.M58 (ebook) | LCC TL230.5.M58 A335 2019 (print) | DDC 629.224–dc23
LC record available at https://lccn.loc.gov/2018002177

Editor: Christina Leaf   Designer: Jeffrey Kollock

Printed in the United States of America, North Mankato, MN

TABLE OF CONTENTS

MONSTER RACE

The monster trucks **rev** their engines. They race around the dirt track. The huge trucks climb a hill and fly over it! They land on a row of junked cars.

Two trucks are side by side. On a sharp corner, one truck leans over. It rides on one tire!

It bounces back down and roars ahead.
It edges across the finish line. The winner!

WHAT ARE MONSTER TRUCKS?

Monster trucks are pickups with strong **suspension** and **oversized** tires. They race on rough **terrain**. These beasts are heavy and tough enough to crush cars. They are awesome and loud displays of power!

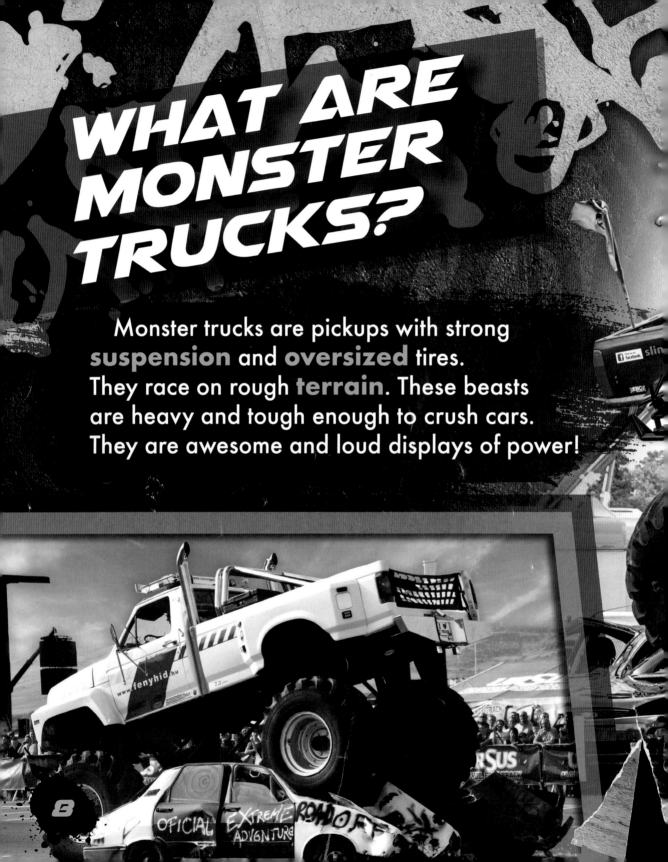

Monster trucks race and jump over **obstacles** on dirt tracks.

wheelie

They do tricks, too. They rise up to do **wheelies**. Some can drive on one wheel! They put on a fun show for fans.

THE HISTORY OF MONSTER TRUCKS

In the 1970s, Bob Chandler liked driving **off-road**. He changed his pickup to handle his rough driving habits. He made a tougher suspension system. He used oversized tires. The truck became known as Bigfoot.

CAR CRUSHERS

Each monster truck tire weighs 800 to 900 pounds (363 to 408 kilograms).

MONSTER TRUCK TIMELINE

Famous monster truck Grave Digger makes its first appearance

1982

1981

Bigfoot drives over and crushes junked cars for the first time

Bob Chandler begins creating Bigfoot

1975

Monster Truck Racing Association (MTRA) forms

Freestyle becomes a common event at monster truck competitions

MID-1990s

Chandler brought Bigfoot to car shows. In 1981, Chandler was recorded driving Bigfoot over junked cars. Bigfoot's huge tires crushed the cars! Soon, other monster trucks were crushing cars, too.

MONSTER TRUCK PARTS

Monster truck parts help them tackle tough terrain. Their tires are 5.5 feet (1.7 meters) tall. Most can steer with all four wheels. Tough suspension systems allow them to climb over cars and land jumps.

MONSTER JUMP

The longest monster truck jump was 237.6 feet (72.4 meters). In 2013, Joe Sylvester did this in Bad Habit.

roll cage

FAST FUEL BURN

A monster truck engine burns about 3 gallons (11 liters) of fuel in one minute.

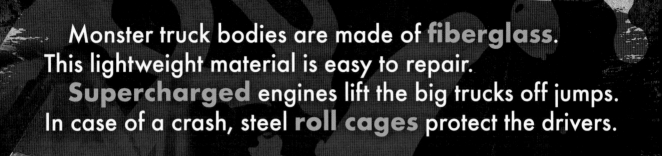

Monster truck bodies are made of **fiberglass**. This lightweight material is easy to repair. **Supercharged** engines lift the big trucks off jumps. In case of a crash, steel **roll cages** protect the drivers.

IDENTIFY A MONSTER TRUCK

body

suspension system

engine

oversized tires

MONSTER TRUCK COMPETITIONS

FREESTYLE FAN FAVORITES

In freestyle, judges score the competitors. Some events let fans decide the winner!

Monster trucks compete in races or **freestyle** events. Races on obstacle courses test trucks' toughness and drivers' skill. In freestyle, monster truck drivers do tricks and stunts to score points. Monster truck events are always exciting!

freestyle

GLOSSARY

fiberglass—a strong material made from very fine glass threads

freestyle—a monster truck event in which drivers do tricks and stunts with their truck to earn points

obstacles—objects that drivers have to go around or over

off-road—on trails or dirt roads

oversized—larger than the usual size

rev—to increase the speed of an engine; the engine gets louder when it revs.

roll cages—strong steel frames inside monster trucks that surround and protect the driver

supercharged—having extra energy or power

suspension—the system of springs, tires, and shocks that cushions a vehicle's ride

terrain—land

wheelies—tricks in which the monster truck rides with the front tires off the ground

TO LEARN MORE

AT THE LIBRARY

Phegley, Kiel. *Monster Jam Official Guidebook*. New York, N.Y.: Scholastic, 2017.

Ransom, Candice. *Monster Trucks*. Lake Elmo, Minn.: North Star Editions, 2017.

Silverman, Buffy. *How Do Monster Trucks Work*? Minneapolis, Minn.: Lerner Publications, 2016.

ON THE WEB

Learning more about monster trucks is as easy as 1, 2, 3.

1. Go to www.factsurfer.com.

2. Enter "monster trucks" into the search box.

3. Click the "Surf" button and you will see a list of related web sites.

With factsurfer.com, finding more information is just a click away.

INDEX

The images in this book are reproduced through the courtesy of: Amy Claxton/ Flickr, front cover, p. 1; Xinhua/ Alamy, pp. 4-5, 7; BONY/ SIPA/ Newscom, p. 6; melis, p. 8; Simon Bratt, pp. 8-9; Ian Shipley SP/ Alamy, p. 10; Michael Doolittle/ Alamy, p. 11, 18-19; Tim DeFrisco/ Getty Images, pp. 12-13; Lee Brown/ Alamy, pp. 14-15; BigfootFan/ Wikimedia Commons, p. 14 (Bigfoot); Kazvorpal/ Wikimedia Commons, p. 14 (Grave Digger); Feliz Miozioznikov, p. 15 (freestyle); Tony Watson/ Alamy, pp. 16-17; ZUMA Press Inc/ Alamy, p. 19 (Grave Digger), 21; PCN Photography/ Alamy, p. 19 (Engine, suspension); Anadolu Agency/ Getty Images, pp. 20-21.